TELLING the TRUTH

TEACHER HANDBOOK

PAGC Third Level Services

TELLING the TRUTH
TEACHER HANDBOOK

Edward Mirasty and Vince Brittain

BIG MOOSE
PUBLISHING

Published by:
Big Moose Publishing
Box 127 Site 601 RR#6
Saskatoon, SK S7K 3J9
www.bigmoosepublishing.com

ISBN: 978-1-989840-55-9
Big Moose Publishing 06/2023

On behalf of the Prince Albert Grand Council, it is an honour and privilege to share the narratives of past Indian Residential School (IRS) Survivors. Using the protocols for collecting and sharing Indigenous elders' stories was instrumental in the gathering of their narratives.

-Edward Mirasty and Vince Brittain

TABLE OF CONTENTS

INTRODUCTION

Tiniki! Thank you for accepting this book as your resource. Following the findings of unmarked graves across Saskatchewan and the country, there is a need to explain the history of marginalization and the social impacts of colonization. For this reason, Grand Chief, Brian Hardlotte of the Prince Albert Grand Council directed the education office to capture stories of IRS survivors. As Kovach (2021) notes, "Research stories uncover the indelible need for human connection, and in that connection, we find ourselves" (p. 175). Through story-telling, we can know the history of Canada and its colonial policies, which is part of the Truth and Reconciliation's Calls to Action. Historically, federal policy was to assimilate Indigenous Peoples through Residential Schools, and it was through that experience that First Nations experienced trauma at the hands of their caregivers. Sharing these narratives is part of the road to decolonization, where IRS survivors can heal and pass on their experiences to the next generation of Indigenous and non-Indigenous Canadians.

The answers to today's issues on and off reserve are not so ambiguous as First Nation leaders, educators, elders, and parents work toward reconciliation. Through their words, a common denominator to many of the social pathologies that impact our communities leads back to former Residential Schools. The phrase being used today is called intergenerational trauma, which is not a new term, but was first described by an Israeli study to describe the experiences of former Holocaust survivors. Duran (2006) states, "not only is the trauma passed on intergenerationally, but it is cumulative. Therefore, there is a process whereby unresolved trauma becomes more severe each time it is passed on to a subsequent generation" (p. 16). To break the cycle of intergenerational trauma is, to tell the truth, and allow the soul wound to heal.

Stories are a traditional way of passing knowledge, history, and culture to Indigenous People. Through that lens, we look inwards to find ourselves as Canadians. Therefore, it is for this reason that collecting IRS stories open and heal the 'soul wound' that has impacted

Canada's Indigenous Peoples. Consciously, we cannot ignore the colonial history that perpetuates ignorance. Ignorance is not bliss, and the social force continues to "induce a collective amnesia" that further enforces colonialism through formal education. Therefore, it is for this reason the Prince Albert Grand Council takes considerable strides to ensure stories our stories survive and lead to Indigenous epistemic knowledge.

This vital initiative proposed by Grand Chief Brian Hardlotte represents a sharing of stories from past IRS survivors and how they endured the trauma from former caregivers of these assimilative institutions. These stories shared by past survivors allow us as teachers, students, and administrators to remember the histories of Residential Schools to bring context to the current socioeconomic conditions of Canada's First Peoples. As a form of reconciliation, it is said that the truth must come before reconciliation can begin.

These stories shared in traditional talking circles are a way to bring healing and move forward in our educational journey as a form of resiliency. To destroy the toxins that infiltrate our communities, families, and ourselves, "Telling the Truth" stories can bring an antidote to stop the cycle of intergenerational trauma. It is the collection of stories in a 'good way' that PAGC education "are well served if they have a pre-existing relationship with the Indigenous communities with whom they wish to research" (p. 170).

Edward H. Mirasty

RESIDENTIAL SCHOOLS: HISTORY/RESILIENCY AUDIENCE/PARTICIPANTS

Elementary/Middle Years Students: Teachers can use this activity as a precursor to teaching about the history of Indian Residential School and the effects of intergenerational trauma.

University/Vocational Students: Teachers can invite first-year university students to a "Telling the Truth" orientation on behalf of the university/college. This activity will be instrumental for any cohort representing specific disciplines (i.e. vocational, psychologists, social workers, mental health workers, and child welfare, etc.)

Note: The instructor will have key terms for students to understand/integrate into their assignments (as part of a recalling exercise):

- Assimilation
- Institutional Racism
- Resiliency
- Indigenization
- Paternalism
- Intergenerational Trauma
- Indigenous People
- Truth and Reconciliation

Teacher Note:

It will be imperative for instructors to know their position and/or social location. (See the **Indigenization Project Sheet** Appendix B). Lastly, refer to the **Perfect Stranger Sheet** (Appendix C), which can be shared prior to/following the Residential School Day Trip.

In Saskatchewan, the LEADS Organization has put out a letter on July 8th, 2021 in response to the unmarked grave sites in the province. See the next page.

LEADS

SASKATCHEWAN LEAGUE OF EDUCATIONAL
ADMINISTRATORS DIRECTORS & SUPERINTENDENTS

RELEASE

For Immediate Release
July 8, 2021

A Statement from the Saskatchewan League of Educational Administrators, Directors and Superintendents

The Saskatchewan League of Educational Administrators, Directors and Superintendents (LEADS) is deeply saddened and troubled by the horrific findings of hundreds of unmarked graves at the former Marieval Residential School on Cowessess and at Muskowekwan First Nation in Saskatchewan, and two other former Residential Schools in Kamloops and Cranbrook, British Columbia.

LEADS shares in the sorrow of all Indigenous Peoples and offers sincere sympathy and condolences to all of the families for the loss of their children.

As the senior educational leaders in Saskatchewan, LEADS is committed to ensuring that all children and youth in classrooms learn the truth about residential schools, the ongoing marginalization if Indigenous Peoples, and the other longstanding consequences of colonization. LEADS promises that our schools will be a place of compassion, honour and respect for all students.

LEADS apologizes for the horrific actions of educators who came before us within the Canadian educational system. LEADS trusts that the present and future actions of LEADS and its members will build equality, trust and respect for all Indigenous peoples.

Chief Cadmus Delorme of Cowessess First Nation has been clear and respectful in calling us to action:

> *"We all inherited this, nobody today created residential schools, nobody today created the Indian Act, nobody today created the 60's Scoop, we all inherited it and we have to acknowledge that people are healing and that people are hurting! Let's do something about it."*

Quintin Robertson, LEADS President
quintin.robertson@gssd.ca
(306) 786-4750

Ben Grebinski, LEADS Executive Director
bengrebinski@saskleads.ca
(306) 539-0451

Kevin Garinger, LEADS President-Elect
kevin.garinger@horizonsd.ca
(306) 682-2558

420–22nd Street East, Saskatoon, SK S7K 1X3
leads@saskleads.ca 306 519 1764
www.saskleads.ca

3

Setting the Stage

Students will be asked to understand the importance of Listening to oral stories and creating a space within their current learning environment. This is taken from Gittelsohn, Belcourt, Magarati, Booth- LaForce, Duran, Mishra, Belone, Blue Bird, (2018)

Listening is an important aspect to reconciling...

As one author notes, "The concept of 'listening to hear' is explored in allyship scholarship (McGloin, 2015). When teachers and students hear stories and different perspectives on racism and colonization, they have to consider how their own perpetuation of colonization affects what is heard, and learning stops if they become paralyzed by guilt and shame... A productive pedagogical approach, therefore, is to build into courses a methodology that reminds students – and teachers – that disease can be a valuable starting point for a more healthy alliance with Indigenous people... Listening – or hearing – what the "other" has to say, in fact, must be a risk-taking venture in order for a change in thought, perception and action to occur. If we are only to hear what is safe or familiar, there will be no conflict, no 'poles of contradiction', no impetus or motivation for transformation." (p. 49)

1. Upon entry, each student will take a walk to a designated seating area that is positioned in a circle where they will be motioned to sit (weather permitting).

   Note: For accessibility, students with wheel chairs will have an open area to sit around the circle. A large tent may help in facilitating an outdoor experience while maintaining social distancing.

2. The instructor(s) will introduce the emcee (local leader) who will introduce the presenters, elders and other key members of the community. They will instruct each participant to turn their cell phones off and to listen and ask questions when prompted by the community representatives.

3. Once the opening prayer has been completed, the elder(s) will explain what the meaning of the prayer was about "to honour the spirits" of the deceased children who were buried at the former Residential School.

4. A local elder (or drum group) will begin with an honour song and upon completion, he/she will sit (in a designated area within the circle) with the group of students.

5. An emcee will share the significance of the Circle and the ethical protocols of sharing information, asking questions; for instance, **talking circles** have been used as a way of building community capacity. As Gittelsohn, Belcourt, Magarati, Booth- LaForce, Duran, B., Mishra, S., Belone, L., Blue Bird (2018) note, "talking circles are a traditional indigenous method of information sharing and decision making used by a group to discuss a topic in an egalitarian and non-confrontational manner," (p. 1).

6. It will be important for the group of students to ask questions after the storytelling as a way to share their perspectives without judgment.

Preparing For Smudge Ceremony

Since the majority of universities/colleges now recognize the indigenous spiritual aspects of this practice, beginning the road to reconciliation would be to immerse themselves in the smudge ceremony. As Gittelsohn, Belcourt. Magarati, Booth- LaForce, Duran, Mishra, Belone, Blue Bird (2018) note, "many universities provide little guidance or training for working in indigenous communities, leaving it up to the researchers to forge relationships themselves and learn or share experiences. In other words, institutionally supported policies or initiatives within universities providing learning opportunities for researchers new to working with indigenous communities are rare," (p. 524).

Thus, allowing communities to share their narrative on the history and impact of Residential Schools. Furthermore, it will be essential for teachers to understand the Perfect Stranger and to refer to page 3 - The Indigenization Project.

Answer: The emcee will begin the meeting with a "smudge ceremony" to purify and cleanse the activity. They will explain the spiritual principles/protocols of the smudge ceremony and its significance for indigenous peoples. Each student will be invited to participate in the smudge ceremony. The elder's helper will circle each participant, burning sweetgrass and waving the smoke toward each student. This cleansing process allows each participant to partake in the purification ceremony. The Reticular Activation System (RAS) will be enhanced with the smudge ceremony's sight, smell, and sound leading up to the presentation/activity.

CREATING A POSITIVE CLIMATE

The morning session of the Residential School Day Trip will involve community members, such as local elders, leaders and program managers (i.e. Social Worker, Education, Mental Health, etc.). It will be during the introduction that a local elder and local leader will emphasize this opportunity to learn about their histories and to have them consider the emphasis of the Truth and Reconciliation (TRC) Calls to Action. Modelling Attributes (Schunk, 2020, p. 141) for both the teacher/student will build self-efficacy for future 'indigenization' activities. Consequently, the experience will build a positive climate for sensitive issues such as the Residential School Legacy. See Fig 1 below.

Note: It is important to ensure schools/institutions select IRS elders who are on the healing journey and would feel safe & comfortable to share their narrative.

Fig. 1

The Reticular Activating System

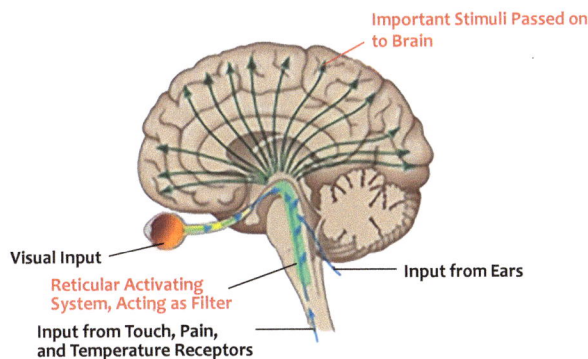

Fig. 1- Reticular formation, Reticular activating system & Types of EEG waves & Phases of sleep from https://www.online-sciences.com/medecine/reticular-formation-reticular-activating- system-types-of-eeg-waves-phases-of-sleep/.

How will you promote a culture in which participation and mistakes are encouraged?
Examples: teaching social-emotional development, using restorative justice protocols
Building Top-Down Emotional Control: **How will you build emotional self-regulation?**

Answer:

1. The emcee will introduce the purpose of the day's events, which is to learn about the Residential School, the intergenerational trauma, and the Resiliency of Indigenous Peoples in bringing back culture, language and ways of knowing.

2. Make a brief welcome and opening remarks on behalf of the Indiginous Storytellers.

   Note: In preparation for any teacher/administrator, here are some important things to think about as you prepare to deliver these activities as taken from the Legacy of Hope Foundation (2018) Guide. (See Resources on page 16)

3. No one can know everything that happened at the Residential Schools. Try not to position yourself as an "expert." Even if you have a connection to the content, try to remain open to the possibility that participants may have more or different knowledge or experiences than you do.

4. There are few generalizations that can automatically apply to all Residential Schools. Each school, in its particular location, under its particular administration, and at a particular time, had unique features. It is important to listen for, recognize, and discuss differences. This should be made clear to participants.

5. Some of the content in these activities deals with difficult subjects and emotional responses may be triggered in participants as a result. It is vital to create a supportive environment when presenting these materials – one in which participants can express their feelings and thoughts openly.

ACTIVITY

Using the Medicine Wheel concept from the Legacy of Hope Foundation. (2018), have students listen to the testimonies from the Elders and complete the Medicine Wheel Chart to help categorize their thoughts as it pertains to the specific quadrant.

When students are in a positive emotional state, the information they learn may be directed by the amygdala (emotional filter) to flow to the prefrontal cortex.

Examples: building emotional awareness; practicing mindfulness, visualization, and stress-reduction techniques; busting stereotypes; teaching students about their brains

Your Plan: Lesson/Unit Elements

Motivation and Perseverance: Which dopamine boosters will be included in your lesson?

Answer: Following the drum/opening prayer, the smudge ceremony will allow for students to build the environment conducive to emotional/spiritual preparedness as they will feel cleansed and ready for the day. Students wishing not to participate in the smudge ceremony will be offered and can pray in their own unique way.

Dopamine Boosters

Dopamine can promote pleasure, decrease stress, and boost curiosity, attention, and motivation. It also contributes to memory formation and retention. Dopamine boosters include music, being read to, humor, interacting with peers, movement, choice, optimism and kindness, gratitude, making correct predictions, and achieving challenges.

Your Plan: Lesson/Unit Elements:

It is said that the honour song will allow for participants to feel empowered with the drum. Indigenous people say the drum is the sound of a heartbeat. For indigenous people, the heartbeat of Mother Earth is the sound that grounds them to the land.

Syn-Naps Brain Breaks

Where can you build in opportunities to shift modes of learning/processing in order to replenish neuro-transmitters and encourage mental manipulation?

Answer: Following the introduction lesson, students will be given a 15-minute break to go for a short break/drink water/washroom. Following the break, the MC will introduce 1-2 elders to share their stories of the Residential School and what the experience was like for them. Each elder will be given 30-45 minutes each to share their narrative of the Residential School experience and shed light on the missing children and those who have passed away from the institution.

Answer: Students will be expected to develop a short essay on a written narrative of at least two perspectives of The Legacy of the Residential School (Using notes from Medicine Wheel) which focuses on the Intergenerational Trauma and the Resiliency. Finally, what can they do as university students on accommodating the TRC's Calls to Action?

See Appendix A.

TRUTH + RECONCILIATION
CALLS TO ACTION

63. We call upon the Council of Ministers of Education, Canada to maintain an annual commitment to Aboriginal education issues, including:

i. Developing and implementing Kindergarten to Grade Twelve curriculum and learning resources on Aboriginal peoples in Canadian history, and the history and legacy of residential schools.

ii. Sharing information and best practices on teaching curriculum related to residential schools and Aboriginal history.

iii. Building student capaccity for intercultural understanding, empathy, and mutual respect.

iv. Identifying teacher-training needs relating to the above.

HELP LINE FOR
RESIDENTIAL SCHOOL SURVIVORS

Indian Residential School Survivors and Family

1-800-721-0066

The Indian Residential Schools Crisis Line is available 24-hours a day for anyone experiencing pain or distress as a result of his or her Residential school experience.

Resources

Allan, B., Perreault, A., Chenoweth, J., Biin, D., Hobenshield, S., Ormiston, T... & Wilson, J. (2018). Pulling Together: A Guide for Teachers and Instructors. Victoria, BC: BCcampus. Retrieved from https://opentextbc.ca/indigenizationinstructors/.

Duran, Eduardo. (2006). Healing the Soul Wound: Counseling with American Indians and Other Native People (Multicultural Foundations of Psychology and Counseling Series). Teachers College Press. Kindle Edition.

Gilson, J., Belcourt, A.. Magarati, M., Booth-LaForce, C., Duran, B., Mishra, S., Belone, L., Blue Bird, V. (2018). Building Capacity for Productive Indigenous Community-University Partnerships. Society for Prevention Research. Retrieved on February 24, 2021 from https://doi.org/10.1007/s11121-018-0949-7

Hansen, J. (2018). Cree elders' perspectives on land-based education: A case study. Brock Education Journal, 28 (1), pp. 74- 91. Retrieved on June 16th, 2021 from file:///Users/edmirasty/Downloads/783-Article%20Text-2705-1-10-20181210.pdf

Hadley, H. (2021). How our Mindset influences the Perception of Pain. Retrieved on August 3, 2021 from https://prezi.com/p/edit/fak5d0mxn4vd/.

Huaman, S., E. (2019). Comparative Indigenous education research (CIER): Indigenous epistemologies and comparative education methodologies. International review of education. Volume 65, pp 163-184.

Kovach, M. (2021). Indigenous Methodologies: Characteristics, Conversations, and Contexts, Second Edition (2nd ed.). The University of Toronto Press. Kindle Edition.

Legacy of Hope Foundation. (2018). Let the truth be told: Indigenous oral testimonies activity guide. Ottawa, ON. Retrieved on June 26, 2021 from file:///Users/edmirasty/Downloads/Let-the-Truth-Be-Told-Guide-2018-V1.44-HR-compressed-1.pdf.

Lemley, C. K., Lee, L. T. (2016). Honoring indigenous teacher education students' stories: Shifting indigenous knowledge from the margins to the center. Journal of American Indian Education, Vol. 55 (2), pp. 28-50.

Morcom, L., Freeman, K. (2018). Niinwi - kiinwa - kiinwi: Building non-indigenous allies in education through indigenous pedagogy. Canadian Society for the Study of Education: Canadian Journal of Education; 41 (3), pp 808-833.

Northern Resource Learning Consortium. Infusing indigenous knowledge into the curriculum: Alberta grades 1-6. Retrieved on July 25, 2021 from https://sites.google.com/arpdc.ab.ca/infusingindigenousknowledge.

Schunk, D. (2018). Learning theories: An educational perspective (8th Edition). Hoboken, New Jersey. Pearson.

Science of Psychology (2018). Amygdala. Retrieved on August 3, 2021 from https://www.thescienceofpsychotherapy.com/glossary/amygdala/.

Tools for Thought.(2020). Listening and learning from elders. The Critical Thinking Consortium.

Truth and Reconciliation Commission of Canada. (2015). Final Report of the Truth and Reconciliation Commission of Canada: Volume One. Toronto, Ontario: Lorimer.

Willis, Judy; Willis, Malana. Research-Based Strategies to Ignite Student Learning . ASCD. Kindle Edition.

Wilson, J., Gobeil, M.(2017). Guitars and makerspace: Examining the experience of First Nations students. Canadian Journal of Learning and Technology. Volume 43(2), pp. 1-16.

APPENDIX A

Activity 1: Review of Residential School Survivors' Narrative

Student Handout – Graphic Organizer – Medicine Wheel

This is a medicine wheel. It is used by some Indigenous Peoples as a representation of the elements of a whole person. These elements are the **physical** (bottom), **intellectual** (left), **spiritual** (top), and **emotional** (right). We will use this as a critical thinking tool to help us better understand Oral Testimony and the experiences of Indigenous Survivors at Residential Schools. Try taking notes from an Oral Testimony and see if you can categorize what is being said into different areas of human experience. Do not worry if you are having trouble categorizing an experience, Just go with what you feel is right.

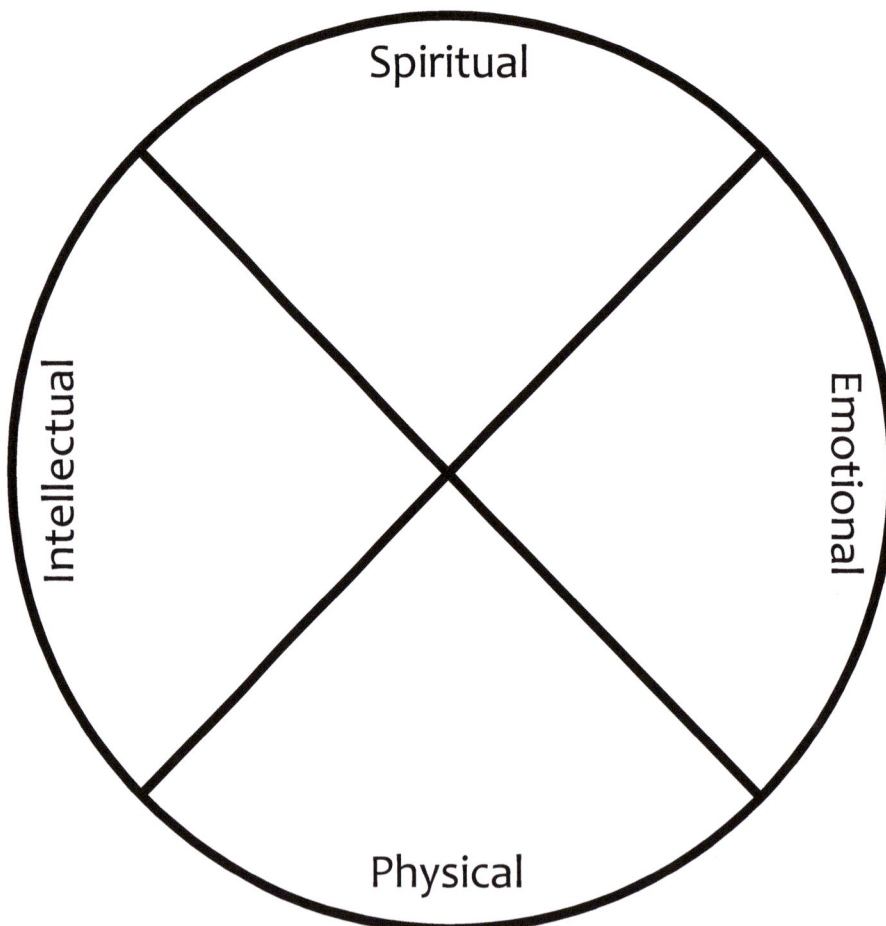

Spiritual

Intellectual

Emotional

Physical

APPENDIX B

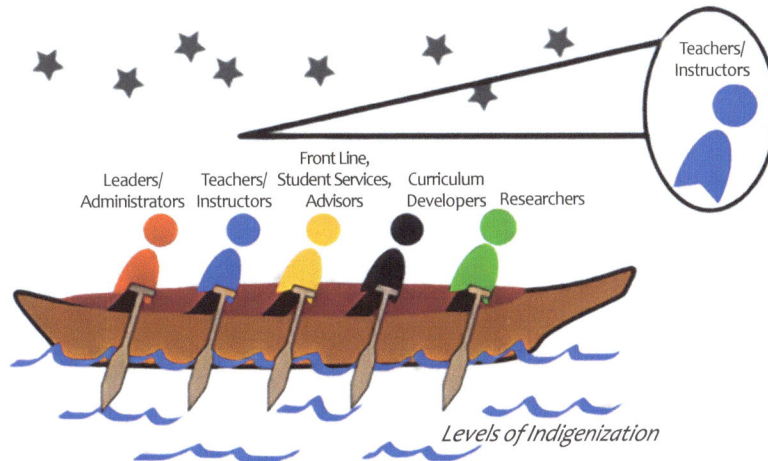

Fig. 0.1 Pulling Together: A Canoe Journey

To help illustrate the process of indigenization by key stakeholders, Allan, Perrault, Chenoweth, Biin, Hobenshield, Ormiston, and Wilson (2018) explain the Indigenization Process:

"The Indigenization Project can be described as an evolving story of how diverse people can journey forward in a canoe (Fig. 0.1). In Indigenous methodology, stories emphasize our relationships with our environment, our communities, and with each other. To stay on course, we are guided by the stars in the sky, with each star a project principle: deliver holistically, learn from one another, work together, share strengths, value collaboration, deepen the learning, engage respectfully, and learn to work in discomfort. As we look ahead, we do not forget our past.

The canoe holds Indigenous Peoples and the key people in post-secondary education whose roles support, lead, and build **Indigenization**. Our combined strengths give us balance and the ability to steer and paddle in unison as we sit side by side. The paddles are the open resources. As we learn to pull together, we understand that our shared knowledge makes us stronger and makes us one.

The perpetual motion and depth of water reflects the evolving process of Indigenzation. Indigenization is relational and collaborative and involves various levels of transformation, from inclusion and integration to infusion of Indigenous perspectives and approaches in education. As we learn together, we ask new questions, so we continue our journey with curiosity and optimism, always looking for new stories to share.

We hope these guides support you in your learning journey. As open education resources, they can be adapted to fit local context, in collaboration with Indigenous Peoples who connect with and advise your institution. We expect that as more educators use and revise these guides, they will evolve over time." (p.12)

APPENDIX C

Knowing Yourself in Relation to Indigenous Peoples:
The Perfect Stranger

Working through unlearning and relearning the collective histories of Canada is an emotional journey. Non-Indigenous teachers and instructors often feel anger, guilt, and shame for not having known about the atrocities levelled against a population in this country. As well, teachers exploring ways to include Indigenous content have to explore and identify their own perceptions of Indigenous identity, along with their personal biases and prejudices. Susan Dion, a Lenapte and Potawatami educational scholar from York University, spent time with non-Indigenous teachers to explore ways to weave Indigenous and Western knowledge systems in a participatory, transformative way (the Braiding Histories project). During her research, Susan realized that teachers' personal biases and prejudices were hindering the way they used or referred to Indigenous pedagogies, such as storytelling.

When teachers take up the task of teaching about Aboriginal people, they are enacting historically structured social forms that organize, regulate and legitimate specific ways of thinking and communicating. The discourse of the romantic, mythical Other is enacted through the teachers. How and what teachers communicate about Aboriginal people is based not on an arbitrary decision, but is established on a long history of how Aboriginal people have been positioned in relationship to non-Aboriginal people. Aware that the discourse of the romanticized, mythical Other is embedded in a teacher's understanding of what it means to teach First Nations subject materials, but simultaneously holding a somewhat contradictory faith in the transformative power of education, I realize that accomplishing change calls for a project that will interrupt the dominant discourse and offer teacher and students alternative ways of knowing.(2009 p. 64)

The teacher's understanding therefore positions the Indigenous person as the "perfect stranger", and generates a hands-off relationship with Indigenous Peoples where Indigenous content is used in a contributive or addictive approach (Goulet & Goulet, 2014 p. 2). This understanding perpetuates a dominant view of Indigenous Peoples and disables the ability to respectfully engage and acknowledge Indigenous world views in transformational learning. It is not only historical omissions that non-Indigenous teachers have to understand, but also how they hold themselves in relationships and interactions with Indigenous Peoples, knowledge systems, and perspectives. Susan Dion explains:

The fear of offending, the fear of introducing controversial subject material, the fear of introducing content

that challenges students' understanding of the dominant stories of Canadian history, all support the claim for the position of perfect stranger. Dominant stories that position Aboriginal people as, for example, romanticized, mythical, victimized or militant Other, enable non-Aboriginal people to position themselves as respectful admirer, moral helper, protector of law and order. (2007 p. 331).

Indigenization can become misguided if educators and instructors are unaware of the ways in which values and beliefs can perpetuate the "perfect stranger", and thus affect meaningful engagement with Indigenous knowledge systems and perspectives in content and practice.

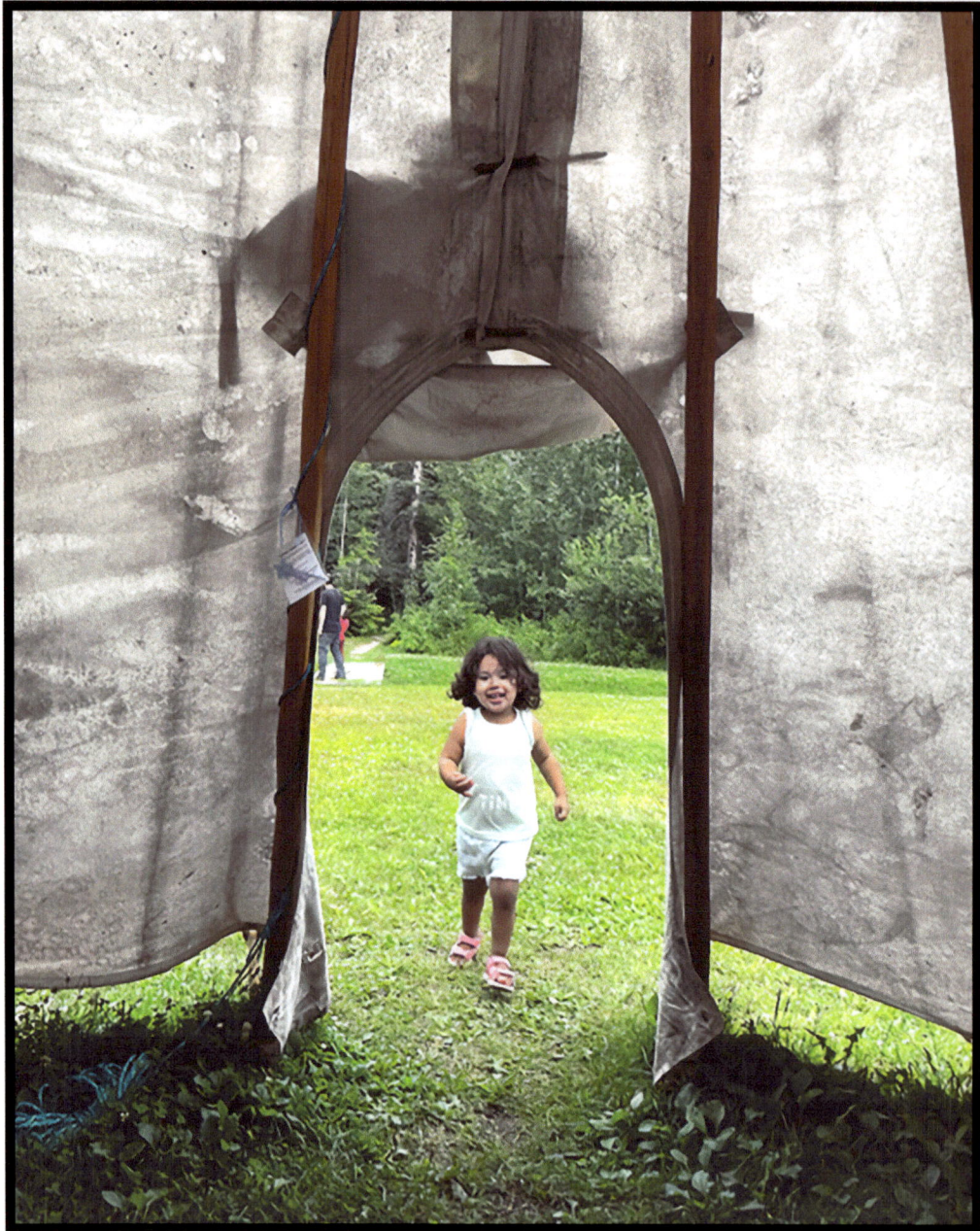

Girl in Photo: Lilly B Mirasty

Indigenous storytelling allows future generations to understand the history, culture, and land-based knowledge of First Nations in Canada.

www.ingramcontent.com/pod-product-compliance
Lightning Source LLC
Chambersburg PA
CBHW061147030426

42335CB00002B/133